# Hip Hop Street Curriculum:

## Keeping it Real

First Edition, First Printing
Copyright 2005 by Jawanza Kunjufu

*(Kiswahili for dependable and cheerful)*

## We recommend classroom use. Volume discounts are available.

*Visit our web site at*
**http://www.AfricanAmericanImages.com**
*or*
*e-mail us at*
**AAI@AfricanAmericanImages.com**

African American Images
Chicago, Illinois

# Contents

# Dear Reader:

I respect you because you did not fall for the lies. Columbus did not discover America, Lincoln did not free the slaves, and Egypt is not in the Middle East. I know you are bored with a Eurocentric, irrelevant curriculum. I also know you have little respect for those teachers who do not respect, like, or care about you. I know you want a curriculum that will connect the school to the streets. For example, if you live in a neighborhood that is poor, filled with crime, drugs, gangs, fatherless children, and crooked police officers, the curriculum should teach you how to improve the conditions in your neighborhood.

*Hip Hop Street Curriculum* is my gift to you. I have listened and learned from you. We now need to listen and learn from each other.


Your brother,

Jawanza Kunjufu

# Tupac

The son of two Black Panther members, Tupac Amaru Shakur was born in New York City on June 16, 1971. His parents had separated before he was born, and his mother moved him and his sister around the country for much of their childhood. Frequently, the family was at the poverty level, but Shakur managed to gain acceptance to the prestigious Baltimore School of the Arts as a teenager. While he was at the school, his creative side flourished, and he began writing raps and acting. Before he graduated, his family moved to Marin City, California, when he was 17 years old. Over the next few years, he lived on the streets and began hustling.

He released his debut album, *2Pacalypse Now* in 1991. The album became a word-of-mouth hit, as "Brenda's Got a Baby" reached the R&B Top 30 and the record went gold. Shakur's profile was raised considerably by his acclaimed role in the Ernest Dickerson film *Juice*, which led to a lead role in John Singleton's *Poetic Justice* the following year. By the time the film hit theaters, 2Pac had released his second album, *Strictly 4 My N.I.G.G.A.Z.* in 1993, which went platinum.

In 1992, 2Pac was arrested for his involvement in a fight that led to the death of a six-year-old bystander by a stray bullet; the charges were later dismissed. 2Pac was filming *Menace II Society* in the summer of 1993 when he assaulted director Allen Hughes; he was sentenced to 15 days in jail in early 1994.

The sentence followed two other high-profile incidents. In October 1993, he was charged with shooting two off-duty police officers in Atlanta. The charges were dismissed, but the following month, he and two members of his entourage were charged with sexually abusing a female fan. In 1994, he was found guilty of sexual assault. The day after the verdict was announced, he was shot in the lobby of a New York City recording studio by two muggers. Shakur was sentenced to four-and-a-half years in prison in February 1995.

He was in jail when his third album, *Me Against the World*, was released in 1995. The record entered the charts at number one, making 2Pac the first artist to enjoy a number one record while serving a prison sentence.

Tupac signed with Death Row Records in late 1995. His Death Row debut, *All Eyez on Me*, was the first double disc of original material in Hip Hop history. It debuted at number one upon its 1996 release and was certified quintuple platinum. His single, "Dear Mama," illustrated that he was capable of sensitivity as well as violence.

Since his death at 26 (September 13, 1996) the following albums have been released: *R U Still Down*, *Better Dayz*, *2Pac Rap*, *Nu-Mixx*, *Klazzics, Resurrection* and *Machiavelli*.

ઌ  ઌ  ઌ  ઌ  ઌ  ઌ  ઌ  ઌ  ઌઌ  ઌ  ઌ  ઌ  ઌ  ઌ

1) What else do you know about Tupac?
2) Describe his music.
3) How do you feel about Tupac?

# Reasons Why Some Believe 2PAC Is Still Alive!!!

1) There were never any pictures released of Tupac in the hospital.

2) The video, "I Ain't Mad At Cha," was released a few days after his death. The video shows Tupac as an angel in heaven.

3) In the song "Life Goes On," Tupac raps about his own funeral.

4) The driver of the car in which Tupac was shot, Suge Knight (executive producer of Death Row Records), didn't show up for questioning about the shooting.

5) A shooting involving Snoop Doggy Dogg occurred close to the release of his album *Doggystyle,* which made Snoop appear more "real" and showed that he really was a gangsta. The shooting gave him respect, and his fans believed what he talked about on the album. Within one week of its release, *Doggystyle* went platinum. Snoop is signed to the same label as Tupac, which is Death Row Records.

6) In interviews prior to the shooting, Tupac talked about how he wanted to stop rapping and being a gangsta. He wanted to get out of the limelight. What is the only way Tupac could completely escape the media spotlight? (Answer: By publicly faking his death.)

7) There are no suspects in the shooting.

8) The press wasn't allowed to attend the funeral, and the funeral was cancelled for unknown reasons.

9) Tupac always wore a bulletproof vest, no matter where he went. Surely he would have worn it to a public event like the Tyson fight.

10) In most of his songs, Tupac talked about being buried. So why was he allegedly cremated the day after he "died?" And since when are corpses cremated the day after death?

11) 2Pac died on Friday the 13th.

12) Las Vegas is a payoff city, meaning all sorts of folks (doctors, the press, lawyers, etc.) are on the take.

13) The white Cadillac containing the assailants was never found. How could this be when Vegas is in the middle of a desert?

14) There's a small Black community on the North side of town. This strip is only about eight blocks long. The attackers were Black. Where did they go? Where did they hide?

15) The Cadillac containing the gunmen passed an entourage of 2Pac's boys, many of them bodyguards. No one gave chase, and there were no witnesses on the street. Why not?

16) The name of 2Pac's next album was *Machiavelli*. Machiavelli was an Italian war strategist who faked his death to fool his enemies. Perhaps 2Pac is doing the same thing.

17) The cover of his next album *R U Still Down?* has 2Pac looking like Jesus Christ. Could he be planning a resurrection?

18) Las Vegas is in the middle of the desert. Why was there no helicopter chase? If someone was to rob a casino, the police would've chased him down with helicopters. Why didn't this happen with 2Pac's assailants?

19) There was no autopsy.

20) There were no ballistic tests.

21) Las Vegas is a mob town. No one gets killed on the strip without getting permission first. Who was calling the shots on this one?

22) 2Pac's vehicle was shot 12 times, but Suge didn't get hit once. He was "grazed" by a bullet. How could 2Pac get shot all those times and Suge not get hit?

23) Suge said that as he drove 2Pac to the hospital, they had a conversation. How bad was 2Pac hit? There are also conflicting stories claiming that Quincy Jones' daughter was in the back of the car and then she wasn't. What's the deal for real?

24) Suge Knight and 2Pac were the only two high profile music industry players with enough nerve to pull off a stunt like faking death.

25) 2Pac's video, "I Ain't Mad At Cha" foretold his death.

26) The memorial services that were open to the public were cancelled in both Los Angeles and Atlanta.

# 50 Cent

Born Curtis Jackson on July 6, 1976 and raised in Southside Jamaica, Queens, 50 grew up in a broken home. 50 Cent (pronounced Fiddy Cent) got his name from a gangster in Brooklyn.

His hustler mother passed away when he was only eight, and his father departed soon after, leaving his grandmother to parent him. As a teen, he followed the lead of his mother and began hustling. The crack trade proved lucrative for 50—until he eventually encountered the law, that is, and began making visits to prison. It's around this point in the mid-'90s that he turned toward rap and away from crime. His break came in 1996 when he met Run-D.M.C.'s Jam Master Jay, who gave him a tape of beats and asked him to rap over it. Impressed by what he heard, Jay signed the aspiring rapper to his JMJ Records label. Eminem signed 50 to a seven-figure contract in 2002.

The willingness to rap openly and brashly and the attention it attracted came back to haunt 50, however. His first post-success brush with death came shortly after the release of "How to Rob" when he was stabbed. Then, on May 24, 2000, just before Columbia was set to release *Power of the Dollar*, an assassin attempted to take 50's life, shooting him nine times with a 9mm pistol while the rapper sat helpless in the passenger seat of a car. One shot pierced his cheek, another his hand, and the seven others his legs and thighs. He survived, but barely. He now always wears a bulletproof vest and drives in a bulletproof car.

During the next two years, 50 returned to the rap underground where he began. In 2003, he released *Get Rich or Die Tryin'*, and the hit was "In Da Club." He formed a collective G Unit of shoes. In 2005, he released *Massacre* which went platinum in less than a week. The CD has sold almost five million copies.

 

&#8667;   &#8667;   &#8667;   &#8667;   &#8667;   &#8667;   &#8667;   &#8667;   &#8667;&#8667;   &#8667;   &#8667;   &#8667;   &#8667;   &#8667;   &#8667;

1)  What else do you know about 50?

2)  Describe his music.

3)  How do you feel about 50?

# Lil' Kim

A native of Bedford-Stuyvesant, Brooklyn, Kimberly Jones was born July 11, 1975. She was raised by her parents until they split up when she was nine years old. She lived with her father until he threw her out of the house when she was a teenager. As a teen, she lived with her friends and, occasionally, on the streets. Eventually, she and her rhyming skills came to the attention of Biggie Smalls, who helped cultivate her career. Smalls helped her become a Junior M.A.F.I.A.

Following the release of *Conspiracy* in 1995, *Hard Core*, was released in late 1996. Lil' Kim's marketing campaign for the album was quite provocative—she wore a skimpy bikini and furs in the advertisements and album cover. Instead of resulting in a backlash, the album became a hit. In 2000, on "Notorious K.I.M.," Lil' Kim rhymed "Never snitch, never send a n_ _ _ _ to jail," but now Kimberly Jones is going to prison for following this "notorious" code of honor.

ॐ ॐ ॐ ॐ ॐ ॐ ॐ ॐ ॐॐ ॐ ॐ ॐ ॐ ॐ ॐ

1) What else do you know about Lil' Kim?
2) Describe her music.
3) How do you feel about Lil' Kim?
4) Did she do the right thing in court?

# Snoop Dogg

Born Calvin Cordozar Broadus on October 20, 1971, in Long Beach, California, "Snoopy," as his mother affectionately called him, later took the name professionally, altering it to Snoop Doggy Dogg, later to Snoop Dogg. Although today a mainstream celebrity, he is a natural survivor of the '90s gangsta rap scene.

Snoop Dogg's early years were marked by frequent bouts with the law, resulting in several jail terms. He later created rhymes about his experiences, which he committed to tape. Eventually, he caught the notice of rapper Dr. Dre, who featured him on his debut solo album, *The Chronic*. Snoop Dogg launched his own career a year later with the debut album, *Doggystyle*.

While recording *Doggystyle,* Snoop Dogg made headlines when he was arrested in the shooting of a gang member. He was eventually acquitted of all charges on grounds of self defense. While the court case would drag on for several years, his first album skyrocketed to number one on the charts, spinning off such hit singles as "What's My Name" and "Gin and Juice".

After the release of his second album, *The Doggfather*, Snoop Dogg created a more widely acceptable image as an A-list show business personality. His first album for Capitol Records was entitled *Paid the Cost to Be da Bo$$* and was released in late 2002. However, he was dragged into the gangsta rap spotlight a year later after surviving a drive-by shooting in Los Angeles perpetrated by three unknown assailants.

Snoop Dogg has appeared in several commercials for AOL and Nokia. Recently he switched to the Geffen label for his latest hit, *Drop It Like It's Hot*.

❧ ❧ ❧ ❧ ❧ ❧ ❧ ❧ ❧❧❧ ❧ ❧ ❧ ❧ ❧ ❧

1) What else do you know about Snoop?
2) Describe his music.
3) How do you feel about Snoop?

# Eve

Born Eve Jihan Jeffers in Philadelphia on November 10, 1978, Eve started singing in her early teens, performing with an all-female vocal quintet. She honed her skills as a rapper in impromptu battles with friends. Before she left high school, she formed a female rap duo called EDGP (pronounced "Egypt"). EDGP performed at local talent shows and club gigs, often to the detriment of Eve's dedication to school. When the group broke up, she went solo and changed her name to Eve of Destruction.

Through some of her friends, Eve scored a meeting with Dr. Dre in Los Angeles and surprised him by turning the meeting into an audition. Dre liked what he heard and signed her to a one-year deal with his new label, Aftermath. Eve next set about establishing a movie career; she made her box-office debut in the Vin Diesel action blockbuster *XXX*, which was released in the summer of 2002. Not long after, she won a prominent supporting role in the Ice Cube comedy *Barbershop*. In early 2003, Eve signed with the UPN network to produce and star in a multiracial sitcom about a fashion designer. Her albums include *Ruff Ryders First Lady*, *Scorpion*, *Eve-Olution*, and *Eve 6*.

❧ ❧ ❧ ❧ ❧ ❧ ❧ ❧ ❧❧ ❧ ❧ ❧ ❧ ❧ ❧

1) What else do you know about Eve?
2) Describe her music.
3) How do you feel about Eve?

# P. Diddy (Puff Daddy)

Sean Combs was born November 4, 1970 in Harlem, the first of Melvin and Janice Combs' two children. Janice was an aspiring model, while Melvin was a notorious street hustler whose lifestyle caught up with him when he was shot dead in Central Park. Sean was only three at the time. For the next ten years, the family continued to live in Harlem, where Sean witnessed firsthand the prime years of Hip Hop's explosive evolution. From block parties to b-boy battles in the park, the seeds of his dream of becoming an entertainer were being sown.

When he was 12, his mother relocated the family to the suburbs of Mount Vernon, New York, where Sean attended Mount St. Michael's Academy, an all-male private school. Legend has it that he earned his nickname when, as a member of the football team, he "puffed" out his chest to make himself look stronger than he actually was—hence the name Puffy.

In 1988, Puffy entered Howard University, where his entrepreneurial drive immediately kicked into high gear. He started out promoting house parties and campus concerts. Reportedly he nurtured a lucrative side business selling term papers and old exams. Two years at Howard were enough for Puffy to realize that it was time to move on to something bigger and better. He dropped out.

He produced multi-platinum albums for Jodeci and for soul-sensation Mary J. Blige, whose debut album, *What's the 411?* is now regarded as the seminal example of Hip Hop/R&B fusion. With the success of those efforts, Puffy then launched his own label, Bad Boy Entertainment. The first artist he signed was a Brooklyn rapper by the name of Biggie Smalls, whose real name was Christopher Wallace.

His next power move would prove to be his greatest to date. He negotiated a $15 million deal to relocate Bad Boy Entertainment to Arista Records. Puffy was given complete creative control and full support by the major label. In return, he more than earned his keep by producing several number one hits with Notorious B.I.G. and Craig Mack.

His clothing line, Sean John, is a multi-million dollar enterprise, he has opened several clothing stores. He has starred on Broadway and ran a marathon for charity. He changed his name to P. Diddy because he wanted something fresh in 2002.

 

&#8540; &#8540; &#8540; &#8540; &#8540; &#8540; &#8540; &#8540; &#8540;&#8540; &#8540; &#8540; &#8540; &#8540; &#8540; &#8540;

1)   What else do you know about P. Diddy?
2)   Describe his music.
3)   How do you like his clothing line?
4)   How do you feel about P. Diddy?

# Foxy Brown

She was born Inga Marchand on September 6, 1979, in Brooklyn, New York. Marchand grew up with another future female rap star, Lil' Kim, in Park Slope, Brooklyn. Naming herself Foxy Brown, after Pam Grier's character. Brown's rapid rise to fame began at the age of 15 when she won a talent contest in Brooklyn.

Her provocative rap on Jay-Z's "Ain't No N_ _ _ _" ("Ain't no n_ _ _ _ like the one I got/sleeps around but he gives me a lot") established her highly sexual and ultra confident persona, which came as a breath of fresh air on the male dominated Hip Hop scene. A major-label scramble for her signature ended when Def Jam Records signed her in March 1996.

Almost overnight Brown has become a powerful female icon, revolutionizing Hip Hop with her sexually explicit lyrics and provocative image. Her albums include *III Na Na*, *Chyna Doll*, and *Broken Silence*.

❧ ❧ ❧ ❧ ❧ ❧ ❧ ❧ ❧❧ ❧ ❧ ❧ ❧ ❧ ❧

1) What else do you know about Foxy Brown?
2) Describe her music.
3) How do you feel about Foxy Brown?

# Jay-Z

Born Shawn Carter on December 4, 1969, and raised in the rough Marcy Projects of Brooklyn, New York, Jay-Z underwent some tough times after his father left his mother before the young rapper was even a teen. Without a man in the house, he became a self-supportive youth, turning to the streets, where he soon made a name for himself as a fledgling rapper.

Known as "Jazzy" in his neighborhood, he shortened his nickname to Jay-Z and did all he could to break into the rap game. Jay-Z made a nontraditional strategic move and decided to start his own label rather than sign with an established label.

Together with friends Damon Dash and Kareem "Biggs" Burke, he created Roc-a-Fella Records, a risky strategy that cut out the middleman so that he could make more money for himself. Of course, he needed a quality distributor, and when he scored a deal with Priority Records (and later Def Jam), Jay-Z finally had everything in place.

Jay-Z reigned over the New York rap scene throughout the late '90s and early 2000s and steadily built up the Roc-a-Fella Records dynasty in the process. The Brooklyn rapper made his splash debut in 1996 and cranked out album after album and hit after hit throughout the decade and into the next. Jay-Z became so successful that Roc-a-Fella, the record label he began with Damon Dash, became a marketable brand itself, spawning a lucrative clothing line (Roca Wear); a deep roster of talented rappers (Beanie Sigel, Cam'ron, M.O.P.) and producers (Just Blaze, Kanye West); a number of arena-packing cross-country tours; and even big-budget Hollywood films (*Paid in Full, State Property*). He says he's going to retire from rapping, continue producing and acquire the Nets basketball team and bring them to Brooklyn.

❧   ❧   ❧   ❧   ❧   ❧   ❧   ❧   ❧❧   ❧   ❧   ❧   ❧   ❧   ❧

1)   What else do you know about Jay-Z?

2)   Describe his music.

3)   How do you feel about Jay-Z?

# Missy Elliott

Born in Portsmouth, Virginia, July 1, 1971, as Melissa Elliott, Missy's professional music career began when Jodeci member/producer Devante Swing signed her group, Sista, to his Swing Mob record label. Unfortunately, Swing Mob Records fell through and along with it the plans for Sista's debut album.

Determined to move forward, Missy turned to longtime acquaintance Timbaland, who happened to be producing some tracks for Aaliyah's *One in a Million* (1996) album. It proved to be a key move for Missy, as the album racked up enormous sales. Soon record execs were knocking on her door. Missy began working with a number of artists as either a songwriter or a vocalist/rapper before finally signing a contract with Elektra in 1996. A year later, *Supa Dupa Fly* hit the streets and soon after went platinum thanks to "The Rain."

In 1999, Missy released with her much-awaited follow-up album, *Da Real World,* an even more ambitious album that featured two mammoth hits—"She's a B_ _ _ _" and "Hot Boyz"— along with an array of often daring collaborations with such unlikely candidates as Eminem. Around this time, she began appearing in TV ads for the Gap and Sprite, proving that not only was she a musical talent, but also an important icon for the era. The cycle repeated itself in 2001 when she released

*Miss E. So Addictive*, again powered by two huge hits: "Get Ur Freak On" and "One Minute Man." Her remarkable popularity continued a year later with her next album, *Under Construction*, and its hit singles, "Work It" and "Gossip Folks." Missy's music machine continued pummeling the charts, with *Under Construction, Pt. II,* and *This Is Not a Test!*

১৩  ১৩  ১৩  ১৩  ১৩  ১৩  ১৩  ১৩  ১৩  ১৩১৩  ১৩  ১৩  ১৩  ১৩  ১৩  ১৩

1)  What else do you know about Missy Elliott?

2)  Describe her music.

3)  How do you feel about Missy Elliott?

# Kanye West

He was born on June 8, 1977, in Atlanta, Georgia to an award winning photojournalist father and an English teaching mother. West was an unlikely sensation and more than once defied adversity. Like so many others who were initially inspired by Run-D.M.C., he began as just another aspiring rapper with a boundless passion for Hip Hop.

Though he did quite a bit of noteworthy production work during the late '90s, it was his work for Roc-a-Fella at the dawn of the new millennium that took his career to the next level. Alongside fellow fresh talent Just Blaze, West became one of the Roc's go-to producers, consistently delivering hot tracks in album after album. He first caught everyone's ear in 2001 when he laced Jay-Z's earth-shaking *Blueprint* album with "Takeover" and "Izzo (H.O.V.A.)."

More high-profile productions followed, and before long word spread that West was going to release an album of his own, on which he'd rap as well as produce. Unfortunately, that album was a long time coming, pushed back and then pushed back again. It didn't help, of course, that West experienced a tragic car accident in October 2002 that almost cost him his life. He capitalized on the traumatic experience by using it as the inspiration for "Through the Wire" (and its corresponding video), which would later become the lead single for his eventually released debut album. That debut album, *The College Dropout* (2004), was continually delayed while West continued to churn out big hits for the likes of Talib Kweli ("Get By"), Ludacris ("Stand By"), Jay-Z ("'03 Bonnie & Clyde"), and Alicia Keys ("You Don't Know My Name").

West earned ten nominations in the 47th annual Grammy Awards, held in early 2005. *The College Dropout* won the Best Rap Album award, "Jesus Walks" won Best Rap Song, and a songwriting credit on "You Don't Know My Name" had West sharing the Best R&B Song award with Alicia Keys.

ဆ ဆ ဆ ဆ ဆ ဆ ဆ ဆ ဆဆ ဆ ဆ ဆ ဆ ဆ ဆ

1)   What else do you know about Kanye West?
2)   Describe his music.
3)   How do you feel about Kanye West?

# Queen Latifah

Queen Latifah was born Dana Owens in Newark, New Jersey, on March 18, 1970. Her Muslim cousin gave her the nickname Latifah—an Arabic word meaning "delicate" or "sensitive"—when she was eight.

In high school, Latifah starred in her school's production of *The Wiz* and began rapping and beat boxing with a group called Ladies Fresh. In college, she adopted the name Queen Latifah and hooked up with Afrika Bambaataa's Native Tongues collective, which sought to bring a more positive, Afrocentric consciousness to Hip Hop.

Latifah began her acting career with supporting and guest roles in *Jungle Fever*, *House Party 2*, *Juice*, and the TV series *The Fresh Prince of Bel Air*. In 1993, she co-starred in the Fox comedy series *Living Single*.

Her older brother Lance was killed in 1992 in an accident on a bike that Latifah had just bought him. She still wears the key to the bike around her neck. Her albums include *All Hail the Queen, Nature of a Sista, Black Reign, Order in the Court,* and *Dana Owens Album.*

❧ ❧ ❧ ❧ ❧ ❧ ❧ ❧ ❧❧ ❧ ❧ ❧ ❧ ❧ ❧

1) What else do you know about Queen Latifah?
2) Describe her music.
3) How do you feel about the Queen?

# Russell Simmons

Russell Simmons was born October 4, 1957, and grew up in the Hollis area of Queens, New York. He spent some of his teen years as a street hustler. He later enrolled in a Harlem college to study sociology. In 1978, he began promoting Hip Hop block parties and club shows around Harlem and Queens, often in tandem with his friend Curtis Walker. Russell became Curtis' manager and also co-wrote his 1979 single "Christmas Rappin'."

Russell quit school to pursue artist management full-time. He formed Rush Productions Company. In 1982, he took on his younger brother Joseph's group as clients, christening them Run-D.M.C. and helped to guide their meteoric rise to stardom over the next few years. Putting up a few thousand dollars, Russell founded the Def Jam record label in 1984 and secured a distribution deal with CBS after some early success with LL Cool J (who recorded Def Jam's first-ever single, "I Need a Beat").

Over the next few years, Def Jam grew into one of the most popular and creatively vital labels in Hip Hop history. In addition to LL Cool J, the label also released acclaimed and influential recordings by Slick Rick, Public Enemy, the

Beastie Boys, EPMD, 3rd Bass, Onyx, and many others. Russell turned the story of Def Jam's founding into the fictionalized film *Krush Groove* in 1985.

In 1991, he began producing the groundbreaking HBO series *Russell Simmons' Def Comedy Jam*, a forum for Black standup comedians to perform their uncensored routines for a wider audience. Among the talents showcased over the series' seven seasons were Martin Lawrence, Chris Rock, Jamie Foxx, Bernie Mac, Cedric the Entertainer, Steve Harvey, D.L. Hughley, and Chris Tucker.

Simmons continued to branch out into other business ventures. In 1992, he launched Phat Farm, a successful men's clothing line; it later spawned a female companion, Baby Phat, which was overseen by onetime supermodel Kimora Lee (who eventually married Simmons in 1999). Simmons is a multimillionaire who gives back to the community. He founded the Hip Hop Summit Action Network to organize rappers to address societal issues.

∽  ∽  ∽  ∽  ∽  ∽  ∽  ∽  ∽∽  ∽  ∽  ∽  ∽  ∽  ∽

1) What else do you know about Russell Simmons?
2) Describe his clothing lines.
3) Is there anyone in the rap industry who has earned more than Simmons?

# Mary J. Blige

Born in the Bronx on January 11, 1971, Mary J. Blige spent the first few years of her life in Savannah, Georgia, before moving with her mother and older sister to the Schlobam housing projects in Yonkers, New York. Her rough life there produced more than a few scars, physical and otherwise. Blige dropped out of high school during her junior year and spent time doing her friends' hair in her mother's apartment and hanging out.

One day, while at a mall in White Plains, New York, Mary sang and recorded Anita Baker's "Caught Up in the Rapture" into a karaoke machine. Mary's stepfather gave the tape to Uptown Records' CEO Andre Harrell. Harrell was impressed with Mary's voice and signed her to sing. Together they developed *What's the 411?*, her debut album. She has worked with Suge Knight, Jimmy Jam, and Terry Lewis. Her albums include *My Life, No More Drama, Share My World, What's the 411?, Love and Life,* and *Mary.*

෨ ෨ ෨ ෨ ෨ ෨ ෨ ෨ ෨෨ ෨ ෨ ෨ ෨ ෨ ෨

1) What else do you know about Mary J. Blige?
2) Describe her music.
3) How do you feel about Mary?

# Nelly

Nelly was born Cornell Haynes, Jr. in Austin, Texas, on November 2, 1974. His childhood was spent in St. Louis. Like so many of his contemporaries, a change in circumstances at a pivotal time changed the course of Nelly's life. When he was a teenager, he was taken away from the streets when his mother moved to nearby suburban University City. It was there that he shifted his attention to playing baseball, storytelling, and writing rhymes. With some high school friends, Nelly formed the St. Lunatics, who scored a regional hit in 1996 with a self-produced single, "Gimmie What You Got."

Nelly caught the attention of Universal, who released his debut album, *Country Grammar*, in 2000. The following summer Nelly returned with his second album, *Nellyville*, and lived up to his self-proclaimed "#1" billing. The album topped the Billboard album chart while the Neptunes-produced lead single, "Hot in Herre," remained atop the singles chart. In all, Nelly impressively held the number one spot on ten different Billboard charts the week of *Nellyville's* release.

His hit streak continued unabated, with "Iz U" (from his stopgap *Derrty Versions* remix album) and "Shake Ya Tailfeather" (from the *Bad Boys II* soundtrack) keeping him in the spotlight while he readied his double-disc *Sweatsuit* project. The separately released double album dropped in the fall of 2004 was preceded by a pair of red-hot singles: "My Place" (a slow jam) and "Flap Your Wings" (a club jam).

જ્ઞ     જ્ઞ     જ્ઞ     જ્ઞ     જ્ઞ     જ્ઞ     જ્ઞ     જ્ઞ     જ્ઞજ્ઞ     જ્ઞ     જ્ઞ     જ્ઞ     જ્ઞ     જ્ઞ     જ્ઞ

1)   What else do you know about Nelly?

2)   Describe his music.

3)   How do you feel about Nelly?

# Hip Hop History

1970    Founder of Hip Hop, Afrika Bambaataa, starts to DJ.

1971    Graffiti and breakin' begin.

1978    Music industry coins the term "rap music."

1979    Kurtis Blow becomes the first rapper to sign with a major label.

1983    Ice T becomes one of first West Coast rappers.

1984    Russell Simmons forms Def Jam Records.

1987    Public Enemy releases their first album.

1990    Tupac becomes a Hip Hop dancer.

1991    NWA's record, "Niggaz4life," becomes the first gangsta rap CD.

1995    Eazy-E of NWA dies of AIDS.

1996    Tupac is killed.

1997    Notorious B.I.G. is murdered.

1999    Lauryn Hill is the first woman nominated for 10 grammy awards.

2004    Hip Hop Summit registers two million youth voters.

# Rap Music

List five gangsta rappers.

List five Africentric (positive lyrics, no cursing) rappers.

List five Christian rappers.

List five female rappers.

Who receives the most radio play? Why?

Could Africentric or Christian rap sell more if the songs received more radio play?

Did you know that four companies—EMI, BMG/Sony, Universal, and Warner—control rap music?

Why are the same 40 songs (out of 5,000) played all day?

Did you know that your brain records more than the beat? Did you know that your brain remembers all the lyrics?

What does "the message is in the music" mean?

Did you know that *Essence* magazine has started a movement titled "Take Back the Music"?

# Rap Videos

- Describe your five favorite videos.

- Describe "Tip Drill."

- Describe "Candy Shop."

- What are your favorite video shows?
  Why?

- Why are the females in the videos usually light-skinned?

- Why do the females wear little clothing?

- Do you think videos promote fancy cars, rims, sex, and liquor?
  Explain.

- Design a video from a rap CD.

# Beat vs. Lyrics

- Nelly releases "Tip Drill" video which shows Nelly swiping a credit card through a woman's butt.

  Should the Black community be offended?

- 50 Cent on *Massacre* releases "Look B_ _ _ _ get in the car."

  Should the Black community be offended?

- Ice T releases *Cop Killer* and the media censors the song.

- NWA releases *"F_ _ _ the Police,"* and the media censors the song.

- Public Enemy releases *Revolverlution,* raps "Free Mumia," and the media censors the song.

- Jadakiss releases "Why," which asks, "why did Bush knock down the towers?" The media censors the song.

- Michael Jackson is forced to change the lyrics of "They Don't Care About Us" because the media feels it is anti-Semetic.

- 2 Live Crew's album, *As Nasty as They Want to Be,* is censored.

- Why does the media censor some songs and not others?

- When will the Black community censor a song?

- Have you noticed how you can hear a song and hum it all day?

Your brain is a brilliant computer!

It stores more than the beat, it records all the lyrics.

# Hip Hop Vocabulary

Write a sentence using each word.

| | |
|---|---|
| Bling-Bling: | big money, diamonds, gold |
| Audi: | to leave, be out |
| 1812: | war, fight (as in the war of 1812) |
| Benjamins: | hundred dollar bills |
| blunt: | marijuana rolled in cigar paper |
| crew: | tight knit friends |
| five finger discount: | stealing |
| glory: | body |
| jimmy hat: | condom |
| off the hook: | fun/spectacular |
| crash: | to fall asleep |
| dog: | a male friend or associate |
| frontin': | pretending |
| ill/illin': | improper behavior |
| jack: | to accost or assault |
| juice: | someone with clout |
| step off: | to leave |
| Up North: | in jail |
| wack: | not original; corny |

List five Hip Hop words that you think most of your classmates don't know.

# Rap Business

- You sell one million CDs at $18.00. How much do you make?

- Distributors make 50 percent. How much do the distributors earn?

- How much do you earn after distributors' take?

- Producers make 40 percent. How much do producers earn?

- How much do you earn after producers' take?

- You have to pay studio and video costs, which are $800,000.

- The IRS takes 40 percent. How much do you earn?

- There are four people in the group. How much does each earn?

- What is the first thing you think they will buy?

- Remember only four percent of rap CDs achieve gold status (500,000 units).

# Hip Hop Fashion

Baby Phat
Blackfokapparel
Bushi
Clark's
Damani Dada
Dupri Styles
FJ560
FUBU
Kalonjiwear
Karl Kani
Lugz
Mecca USA
Napp
No Limit
Outkast Clothing
Parasuco
Phat Farm
Roc-A-Fella
Sean John
Skecher's
Timberlands
Triple 5 Soul
Vokal
Wally's
Wu-wear

# Hip Hop Magazines

*Beatdown,* rap's first newspaper

*Don Diva*

*FEDS*

*FELON*

*Front*

*Mo' Cheez*

*Murder Dog*

*One Nutt*

*Rap Pages*

*Rap Sheet*

*Rap-up Magazine*

*Right On Magazine*

*Stress*

*The Fader*

*The Source,* first Hip Hop magazine

*Trix* (UK)

*URB*

*Vibe*

*XXL*

# The N Word

- The Latin word for Black.

- During slavery and Jim Crow, it was used by Whites to insult African Americans. It was the most negative word to describe a person.

- If African American adults had taught you your history and culture, you would have a better understanding.

- Unfortunately they did not, so some Hip Hop youth can be heard saying "Wassup, my N_ _ _ _ _?"

- Hip Hop culture has turned the most negative word into a term of endearment: "My N_ _ _ _ _."

- Somehow you know enough about the history of the word to stop others outside the race from using it. You also know enough about the word to use it against a brother or sister you don't like, which is the same way Whites used it 200 years ago. "I hate you Black N_ _ _ _ _." "N_ _ _ _ _ you ain't s_ _ _."

☙ ☙ ☙ ☙ ☙ ☙ ☙ ☙ ☙ ☙ ☙ ☙ ☙ ☙ ☙ ☙

1) When people outside your race hear you use the word, are they influenced to use it?

2) Do you think you owe your elders the courtesy and respect not to use it?

3) Do you think you have the right to continue to use the word?

# The B Word

- Why do so many rappers call Black women b_ _ _ _?

- Is your mama, sister, or girlfriend a b_ _ _ _?

- Why do some Black women buy rapper's CDs who call them a b_ _ _ _?

- Why do some Black women wear jewelry with the word b_ _ _ _ on it?

- Do some Black women like being called b_ _ _ _?

- What is sexism?

- Can a brother be against racism but support sexism?

- What does it mean to run a "train" on a woman?

# Pimp

"I don't know what you heard about me, but you can't get a dollar out of me. No cadillacs, no perms, you can't see that I'm a muthaf_ _ _ _ _ pimp"—50 Cent

The dictionary defines a pimp as a man who manages the daily work of a prostitute and takes a percentage (if not all) of her earnings. A "stable" contains all the prostitutes who work for the pimp.

❧  ❧  ❧  ❧  ❧  ❧  ❧  ❧  ❧❧  ❧  ❧  ❧  ❧  ❧  ❧

1) Do you want to be a pimp?

2) Do you want someone to pimp your sister, girlfriend, or mama?

3) What is the difference between Black men being pimps and how slaveowners treated Black women during slavery?

4) Do Black men hate Black women?

5) How can Black women avoid being pimped?

# Tattoos

The tattoo is a staple in Hip Hop culture. No one gets tatted up like a rapper. Arms, backs, chests, hands—all covered with intricate body art, telling life's stories, honoring the dead and the living, making statements, displaying artistic images, or reppin' a crew. Many rap so they don't have to go to jobs and cover up their tattoos.

Once you've decided to get a tattoo, you have to find the right tattoo artist. This is a person who will stick you with needles and ink, so make sure you do some investigating. Ask around and do your homework. It's not just about price—sanitation and cleanliness are key here. You want to see fresh latex gloves, alcohol, antibacterial soap, brand new sterilized needles, individual ink caps, and plastic-covered sterile instruments. Dirty needles can cause hepatitis and AIDS, so make sure that the tattoo artist runs a clean and sanitary shop.

The first step to body art is outlining, which is painful. The pain dissipates as the location gets numb. Next is shading and/or coloring (depending on skin tone). Color is more expensive than just doing black and gray, and it takes longer to heal and needs more touch-up work later.

After the tattoo is done, make sure to follow the aftercare instructions. Be prepared to care for this new addition to your body. Tattoos are like open wounds, so you have to treat them like that. Use A&D ointment for a week and then Vaseline Intensive Care lotion or Jergens for a week. Don't pick at the tattoo, and don't swim for two weeks.

Black henna tattoos can cause significant allergies and rashes, leading to renal (kidney) failure and even death in those who are sensitive to the ingredients. These types of tattoos have appeared particularly dangerous to young children.

There are four methods to remove tattoos, including: surgery to cut the tattoo away; dermabrasion, or sanding the skin with a wire brush to remove the epidermis and dermis layers; salabrasion, or using a salt solution to soak the tattooed skin; and scarification, or removing the tattoo with an acid solution to form a scar in its place.

Body piercing also presents the risk of chronic infection, scarring, hepatitis B and C, tetanus, and skin allergies to the jewelry that is used.

❧   ❧   ❧   ❧   ❧   ❧   ❧   ❧   ❧❧   ❧   ❧   ❧   ❧   ❧   ❧

1) Do you want a tattoo?
2) Do you have a tattoo?
3) Was it done safely?
4) Do you know someone who has had problems with their tattoo?

# Video Games

- "Doom 3"

- "Grand Theft Auto"

- "Gunslinger Girls, Vol. 2"

- "Half-Life 2"

- "Halo 2"

- "Hitman: Blood Money"

- "Manhunt"

- "Mortal Kombat: Deception"

- "Postal 2"

- "Shadow Hearts"

ନ୍ତ ନ୍ତ ନ୍ତ ନ୍ତ ନ୍ତ ନ୍ତ ନ୍ତ ନ୍ତ ନ୍ତନ୍ତ ନ୍ତ ନ୍ତ ନ୍ତ ନ୍ତ ନ୍ତ ନ୍ତ

1) Which games have you played?
2) Write a paragraph about each of the games you've played.
3) Do you believe games can shape behavior?

# Advertising

SPINNERS & FLOATERS

C.R.E.A.M. - FLOATER
· SUV - 22, 24, 26"
· CAR - 20, 22"

ESINEM - FLOATER
· CAR - 18, 20, 22"
· SUV - 22, 24, 26"

BELLAGIO - SPINNER
· SUV - 20, 22, 24, 26"
· CAR - 18, 19, 20, 22"

TRUMP - SPINNER
· SUV - 22, 24, 26"
· CAR - 18, 19, 20, 22"

SPINE - SPINNER
· CAR - 20, 22"
· SUV - 22, 24, 25"

*300C on 22" SHORELINE Wheels
with matching SHORELINE Grille*

ESINEM · CAR - 18, 20, 22"

ONE PIECE

SHORELINE · SUV - 24" · CAR - 16, 19, 20, 22"

1)  What is being advertised?
2)  Do you get the woman in the ad when you buy the wheels?
3)  Should your car note exceed your rent?
4)  Why are there more luxury cars in the ghetto than most suburbs?
5)  How should females feel about this advertisement?
6)  Is this sexism?

# Did You Know?

- 300,000 men are raped annually in prison. African men and women are 12 percent of the national population but 60 percent of the prison population.

- Insurance companies require $5 million worth of coverage for a rap concert. Many arenas refuse to book rap artists.

- Seventy percent of rap music is "legally" bought by White teenagers.

- Hip Hop produced more Black millionaires than the civil rights movement. It is a $10 billion industry.

- Hip Hop is more than music. It includes clothing, hairstyle, dancing, language, graffiti, tattooing, sexuality, values, and attire.

- Mercedes, Lexus, Cadillac, Rolls Royce, Jaguar, and Bentley are the most frequently mentioned cars on rap CDs and videos.

- Most females (extras) on music videos work 12 plus hours but only make $100.00.

- Snoop started out making $6.00 per hour bagging groceries.

- Biggie said, "If I wasn't in the rap game, I'd probably be knee deep in the crack game. Either you slingin' crack rock or you got a wicked jump shot."

- Rap music is the second most popular music. Rock is first, R&B is third, followed by Country, Pop, Religious, Classical, and Jazz.

- Although rappers appear gangsta, many grew up in middle-class homes and attended private schools.

- Seventy percent of African American females graduate from high school while only 50 percent of African American males graduate.

- The government passed a Gangbusters bill which increases jail time and encourages the death penalty. A gang is defined as a group of five. A gang member is anyone with gang tattoos or who wears certain colors.

- Can you imagine working at the following company? Its 500 employees have the following statistics: 29 have been accused of spousal abuse, seven have been arrested for fraud, 19 have been accused of writing bad checks, 117 have bankrupted at least two businesses, three have been arrested for assault, 71 cannot get a credit card due to bad credit, 14 have been arrested on drug-related charges, eight have been arrested for shoplifting, 21 are current defendants in law-suits, 84 were stopped for drunk driving. Can you guess which organization? It's the 535 members of the 108th United States Congress.

- A first grade teacher in Biloxi, Mississippi, held a costume party for her class. One little boy came dressed as a pimp, complementing another little girl who was made up to be a whore.

- Some stores are promoting bulletproof vests to African American males.

# Civil Rights vs. Hip Hop

- What is the civil rights agenda for the 33 percent of African American adults and 50 percent of African American youth who live below the poverty line?

- Who produced the most millionaires, civil rights or Hip Hop?

- Describe what went down between Outcast and Rosa Parks.

- How did you feel about Cedric's comments in *Barbershop* about civil rights leaders?

- What could the Hip Hop community learn from civil rights?

- What could the civil rights community learn from Hip Hop?

# Crack

- America spends $1 trillion on drugs annually.

- Sixty-two percent of all illegal drug users are White. Sixty-four percent of drug convictions are Black and Hispanic. What explains the difference?

- Watch *Godfather I* and the scene where the Godfather did not want to sell drugs. He knew it would land in the White community, but he was vetoed by the other four family members, who said the "darkies are animals and deserve to die."

- If there is war on drugs, why don't they lock up White users rather than minor playing Black dealers?

- Why does five grams of crack receive a five-year mandatory sentence when 499 grams of cocaine receives probation or a warning?

- Which is cheaper, crack or cocaine?

- Which race has the cocaine?

- Which race has the crack?

# Drug Deaths

- Which drug kills the most: nicotine, alcohol, cocaine, or heroin? (The answer can be found on page 134.)

- Do you smoke? How frequently?

- Do you drink alcohol? What do you drink?

- Does smoking lead to drinking?

- Does using legal drugs encourage the use of illegal drugs?

- Should we legalize heroin, cocaine, and marijuana to reduce deaths, crime, and profit?

# Liquor

- Did you know African Americans are only 12 percent of the population but buy 38 percent of the liquor?

- Liquor companies view youth as their growth market.

- Did you know that when Busta Rhymes and P. Diddy rapped "Pass the Courvoisier," sales increased 20 percent?

- Advertisers use rappers to increase liquor sales.

    Rakim    —    Hennessey

    Dr. Dre    —    Coors

    Lil' Jon    —    Cognac

- They know African Americans also like

| | |
|---|---|
| Alcopops | Phat Boy |
| Power Master | Crazy Horse |
| Mike's Hard Lemonade | Smirnoff Ice |
| St. Ides | Swedka |
| Camus 4u | Lucky Nites |
| Mojito | Royal Ice |

- Review Hip Hop magazines and count the liquor ads. Listen to rap CDs and note when they mention liquor. Watch videos and observe when liquor is present.

- Do you drink? If so, what do you drink? How frequently?

- How many liquor stores are in your neighborhood?

- How did Salem Baptist Church in Chicago close down all the liquor stores in their neighborhood?

# Rappers Playin' the Dozens

| ARTIST | SONG | YEAR | TARGET | MOTIVE | BRUTAL BARS |
|--------|------|------|--------|--------|-------------|
| 50 Cent | "Back Down" | 2003 | Ja Rule | To strip one of Hip Hop's most successful artists of any remaining credibility | "You's a poptart sweetheart, you soft in the middle/ I eat you for breakfast, the watch was exchanged for your necklace." |
| Jadakiss | "Freestyle | 2001 | Beanie Sigel | Response to Beanie's "Empire Strikes Back Freestyle" | "N_ _ _ _ _ can't stand you Sigel/ Your flow is mine anyway, so don't bite the hand that feeds you." |
| Beanie Sigel | "Empire Strikes Back Freestyle" | 2001 | Jadakiss | Tired of 'Kiss and D-Block throwing subliminal rocks at the Roc. Beans unleashed the beast. | "What's funny Jason, really think you grimy too/Now everybody liked you better in that shiny suit." |

| ARTIST | SONG | YEAR | TARGET | MOTIVE | BRUTAL BARS |
|---|---|---|---|---|---|
| Nas | "Ether" | 2001 | Jay-Z | Response to Jay-Z's "Takeover" | "When these streets keep callin', heard it when I was asleep/That this Gay-Z and Cock-A-Fella Records wanted beef." |
| Jay-Z | "Takeover" | 2001 | Nas | Response to Nas' claim, in the song "Stillmatic," that Jay blew up only after using a Nas sample of the chorus of his single "Dead Presidents" | "So yeah, I sampled your voice, you was usin' it wrong/ You made it a hot line, I made it a hot song." |

| ARTIST | SONG | YEAR | TARGET | MOTIVE | BRUTAL BARS |
|--------|------|------|--------|--------|-------------|
| 2Pac | "Hit 'Em Up" | 1996 | Notorious B.I.G. | 'Pac held Biggie and Puffy responsible for his being shot and robbed at Quad Studios in 1995. | "First off, f_ _ _ your b_ _ _ _ and the click you claim/Westside when we ride come equipped with game/You claim to be a player but I f_ _ _ _ _ your wife/We bust Bad Boy's n_ _ _ _ _ f_ _ _ _ for life." |

# Willie Lynch Letter

Gentlemen, I greet you here on the banks of the James River in the Year of Our Lord 1712. First, I shall thank you, the gentlemen of the colony of Virginia, for bringing me here. I am here to help you solve some of your problems with slaves.

Your invitation reached me on my modest plantation in the West Indies while experimenting with the newest and still oldest methods for control of slaves. Ancient Rome would envy us if my program is implemented. As our boat sails south on the James River named for the illustrious King James whose Bible we cherish, I find enough to know that your problem is not unique.

While Rome used cords of wood as crosses for standing human bodies along the old highways in great numbers, you are here using the tree and rope on occasion, I caught the whiff of a dead slave hanging from a tree a couple of miles back. You are not only losing valuable stock by hangings, you are having uprisings. Slaves are running away. Your crops are sometimes left in the field too long for maximum profit. You suffer occasional fires. Your animals are killed.

Gentlemen, you know what your problems are. I do not need to elaborate. I am here to provide a method of controlling your black slaves. I guarantee every one of you that installed correctly it will control the slave for at least 300 years. My method is simple. Any member of your family or any overseer can use it.

I have outlined a number of differences among the slaves and I take these differences and make them bigger. I use fear, mistrust, and envy for control purposes. These methods have worked on my modest plantation in the West Indies and they will work throughout the South.

Take this simple little list of differences and think about them. On the top of my list is age, but it is there only because it starts with the letter A. The second is color or shade. There is intelligence, size, sex, size of plantation, attitude of owners, whether the slave lived in the valley, on the hill, east, west, north, south, has fine or coarse hair or is tall or short.

Now that you have a list of differences, I shall give you an outline of action. But before that I shall assure you that distrust is stronger than trust and envy is stronger than adulation, respect, or admiration. The black slave, after receiving this indoctrination, shall carry on and become self-refueling and self-generating for hundreds of years, maybe thousands. Don't forget, you must pitch the old black versus the young black male and the young black male against the old black male. You must use the dark skinned slaves versus the light skinned slaves and the light skinned slaves versus the dark skinned slaves. You must use the female versus the male and the male versus the female. You must also have your servants and overseers distrust all blacks, but it is necessary that your slaves trust and depend on us. They must love, respect, and trust only us.

Gentlemen, these kits are your keys to control. Use them. Have your wives and children use them. Never miss an opportunity. My plan is guaranteed, and the good thing about this plan is that if used intensely for one year, the slaves themselves will remain perpetually distrustful.

❧ ❧ ❧ ❧ ❧ ❧ ❧ ❧ ❧❧ ❧ ❧ ❧ ❧ ❧ ❧

1) How is the Willie Lynch Syndrome being expressed today?
2) How can we break this cycle?

# Why We Hate Each Other

**Stage I**         Slavery                    1620-1865

Chains around the wrists and ankles.

**Stage II**        Self-Hatred                1712

Willie Lynch writes a letter teaching slaveowners how to make slaves look for differences. Chains around the wrists, ankles, and the mind.

**Stage III**       Jim Crow Segregation       1865-1954

Separate schools and facilities for African Americans. Chains around the mind.

**Stage IV**        1980-Present

Four companies take over rap music (EMI, Sony/BMG, Universal, and Warner). They realize that if they choose the 40 most negative songs and play them all day, they will control your mind.

# Killing Exercise

Mr. Jones is the adult coordinator of the South Central LA Gang Class, a ten-week course for gang members that are in juvenile detention. The students are first asked to write their own obituary along with a letter to their mothers explaining why it was necessary for them to die for the gangs.

The most significant part of the class is the exercise called "The Kill." Mr. Jones writes on the chalkboard the word "kill" and then he says, "Now, I want each of you to give me a real good reason to kill somebody." The words are barely out of his mouth when hands begin to jab the air. Jones nods at one of the kids who replies, "For the f_ _ _ of it." Jones turns back to the blackboard, writes the words and says "Ok, for the f_ _ _ of it. Let's have another reason."

Another student suggests, "Put in work for the hood." Jones writes again and says, "Ok, that's a good reason." Next students says, "Cause he's my enemy." "Yea, that's righteous," says Jones and prints quickly, "an enemy." Another student calls out, "For revenge." "Yea, let's get that one down. That's a good one— revenge." "Cause he said somethin' wrong." Jones, needing clarity, asked, "You mean like 'dissed you?'" "Naw, just wrong. Like you know, wrong." Jones pursued a definitive answer. "Because he said something wrong and now you got to smoke 'em for it right"? "Yea." The kid slouches back in his chair, grinning. He is clearly pleased with himself for having made his thoughts so perfectly understood.

Jones writes the words on the board then turns back to face the kids. He says, "Come on, let's get some reasons up here. Y'all supposed to be such tough dudes. Let's go." Now the answers begin to come quickly: "Cause he looked at me funny." "Gimme that mad dog look." "Cause I don't like him." "Cause he wearing the wrong color." "Cause he gonna hurt a member of my family for money."

Jones just nods his head, scribbling furiously on the blackboard. "So I can jack somebody for dope." "Cause he give me no respect." "Cause he a disgrace." "He a buster." "For his car." "Cause he try to get with my lady." "Cause he a spy in my hood." "In self-defense." "Cause he try to jack you and take yo' sh_ _ for a nickel" "For the way he walk" "If he got somethin' I want and he don't wanna give it to me" "Cause I'm a lock" "For his association" "Cause he call me a baboon—dissed me." "Cause he f_ _ _ with my food—you know, like took one of my french fries."

"Cause I don't like his attitude." "Cause he say the wrong things—he woofed me." "Cause I'm buzzed—you know like high and bent." "Just playin' around." "Cause he f_ _ _ _ _ up in the barber shop."

Jones chuckles as he writes down, "F_ _ _ _ _ up your hair, huh? Well I can understand that." The reasons keep coming. "Cause he a snitch." "Cause he hit up my wall—crossing out names and sh_ _ writing RIP." "If a lady don't give me what I want—you know, the wild thing." "Cause they ugly." "Cause he try to run a con on me."

All of the reasons are on the board in three neatly lettered rows. Mr. Jones steps back to survey the list for a moment and nods his head. Then he turns to look at the kids again and says, "Ok, now which of this sh_ _ would *you* die for?" There is a moment of utter silence. The air seems to freeze with the combined stares of shocked students. Jones stands quietly, staring back at them, then challenges them, "Aw, come on now. If all y'all can kill for somethin', y'all better be ready to die for it. So let's hear it. Which of these reasons you gon' die for? "

One of the kids says "Hell you can erase all that sh_ _". "No let's go point by point," Jones responds. He continues the challenge. Back at the blackboard Jones examines the list. "See what we got here. Ok. Who's gonna die for the f_ _ _ of it?"

As Jones goes over each item, they erase all but three that they would kill for. They agreed they would die for their family, self-defense, and the gang. Jones then says, "Let me tell you somethin', you can be down for your hood. You can go to jail for your hood. You can die for your hood. If you do, if you die, you know what happens, nothin'. Nothin' changes. The beat goes on. All your dead homeboys, even they don't mean diddly because nothin' changes."

Then Mr. Jones puts on the board the words "irrational" and "normal." He says most normal people have a kill – die equation. What they would kill for is what they would die for. For an irrational person, there's no relationship in the kill-die equation. One of the younger kids, the one who was ready to kill the barber for a less than satisfactory haircut, pipes up, "How many reasons was on that black board?" Jones says, "Y'all gave 37 reasons to kill." The kid shakes his head and says, "Thirty-seven is a big a_ _ number." He agrees with the student. "Yea it is, and if you got more than two reasons then you're more than irrational. You're crazy."

∞　∞　∞　∞　∞　∞　∞　∞　∞∞　∞　∞　∞　∞　∞　∞

1) Are you sane or crazy?
2) Why would you kill someone?

# Why Do We Fight Each Other?

- Do you hate yourself?

- Do you hate Black people?

- Do you want attention?

- Do you want to be loved?

- How do your friends and family resolve conflict?

- Do you have low self-esteem? Do you know God? Your history? Your talents? Your purpose in life?

- Do you think manhood/womanhood is physical rather than mental and spiritual?

- What is the influence of television, video games, gangs, and rap music on your life?

- Are you frustrated because you have not experienced academic success?

- Do you feel fighting is your best and only strength?

- Are you mad because you are poor, have an absent father, and/or live in a slum neighborhood?

- Do you feel confident about your future?

- Do you feel your teachers and parents are weak?

# Stanley "Tookie" Williams

Stanley "Tookie" Williams (born 1954) was the founder, along with Raymond Washington, of the Crips, a Los Angeles youth protection organization that grew into one of the most widely-known and notorious street gangs. "Tookie," as he is still known, was convicted on four counts of murder by the State of California in 1981 and is currently on death row in San Quentin State Prison. He maintains his innocence. He has since denounced his life and role as a gang leader and writes from prison about the harmful effects of gang life.

Williams has been nominated for the Nobel Prizes for peace and literature. He has written a series of children's books that have been popular around the world for their anti-violence message and helped to broker a "truce" between the Bloods and Crips. The State of California is considering clemency for Williams. His web site, "Internet Project for Street

Peace," provides a forum for kids at risk from different parts of the world to achieve literacy and share alternatives to violence. He has become an international sensation.

In 2004, a television movie about him, *Redemption*, was released. Jamie Foxx starred as Williams. The film portrays Williams as a menacing young man filled with rage and hate who transforms into a reflective man of letters, working from his cell to promote peace and save lives. Some may see the film's focus on Williams' redemption as a dramatic argument against the death penalty.

ॐ ॐ ॐ ॐ ॐ ॐ ॐ ॐ ॐॐ ॐ ॐ ॐ ॐ ॐ ॐ

1) What else do you know about Stanley "Tookie" Williams?

2) What do you think about his transition from Crip to peacemaker?

3) How do you feel about Stanley "Tookie" Williams?

# Gangs and Safety

- Is your greatest challenge academics, or walking to school safely?

- Some students drop out because they do not feel safe walking to school in gang neighborhoods.

- Why do some people feel gangs are their family?

- Are gangs a result of Black men not doing their job?

- You can avoid gang problems if you join an athletic team.

- You can reduce gang problems with a part-time job or by choosing a different walking route.

- Have you told any adult that you need protection?

- Is there a relationship between Willie Lynch and the gang problem?

- How hard is it to leave a gang?

- What gangs are in your neighborhood?

- Do you feel safe?

- **I beg you, do not drop out of school because you don't feel safe. Talk to an adult you respect in your school or community. God has a great plan for your life!**

# Hip Hop Summit Action Network

- HSAN seeks to foster initiatives aimed at engaging the Hip Hop generation in community development issues related to equal access to high quality public education and literacy, freedom of speech, voter education, economic advancement, and youth leadership development.

- HSAN sponsored successful Hip Hop summits in New York, Los Angeles, Detroit, Atlanta, Chicago, Houston, Miami, Washington, D.C., Kansas City, Philadelphia, Seattle, Birmingham, and Dallas, providing a national template for engaging the Hip Hop generation in community-building dialogues.

- On August 14, 2003, the Philadelphia Hip Hop Summit registered more than 11,000 voters, the largest number of young new voters ever registered at a single Hip Hop event in the United States.

- HSAN's Hip Hop Team Vote, along with the WWE's SMACKDOWN YOUR VOTE, announced a voter registration campaign of "Two Million More," with the objective of registering two million 18–30 year-olds to vote in the Presidential election.

- The Detroit Hip Hop Summit mobilized more than 17,000 youth participants at the Cobo Arena for leadership development.

- HSAN mobilized 100,000 New York City public school students and top Hip Hop recording artists to a protest rally at City Hall, which resulted in Mayor Bloomberg restoring $300 million in proposed cuts to the New York City public school budget.

- HSAN sponsored free concerts at the Superbowl game and the NBA all-star game. The only requirement was that you had to register to vote. This strategy registered thousands.

                               

1) Describe five positive activities sponsored by rappers.

# Writing Campaign

- Let's write letters to judges asking why crack receives greater punishment than cocaine.

- Let's write letters to the media and the police chief letting them know the location of the crack houses.

- Let's write letters to the police chief informing them which police officers are on the "take."

- Let's write letters to the politicians demanding jobs, recreation, employment, and training.

- Let's write letters to the media and politicians about stores selling liquor, cigarettes, and drug paraphernalia to minors.

Drug Enforcement Agency, 2401 Jefferson Davis Highway, Alexandria, VA 22301

Congressional Black Caucus, 2236 Rayburn House, Washington, DC 20515

U.S. Department of Justice, 950 Pennsylvania Avenue, N.W., Washington, DC 20530

ABC, 7 W. 57th St., New York, NY 10023

NBC, 30 Rockefeller Plaza, New York, NY 10112

CBS, 524 W. 57th St., New York, NY 10019

Fox, 1211 Avenue of the Americas, New York, NY 10036

EMI, 27 Wrights Lane, London W855W

Universal, 2440 Sepulveda, Los Angeles, CA 90064

Warner, 75 Rockefeller Plaza, New York, NY 10019

Sony/BMG, 550 Madison Ave., New York, NY 10022

Viacom, 1515 Broadway, New York, NY 10036
(they own BET/VH1/MTV)

# Hip Hop Math

1) How many NBA teams make the playoffs? What is the maximum number of games the teams will play before one is declared champion? What is the minimum number of games the teams will play?

2) La Bron James took 14 three-point shots and made six. What is his percentage?

3) Shaq took 20 free throws and made seven. What is his percentage?

4) Nike makes shoes overseas for $2.38 and sells them for $119.95. What is their profit?

5) You make $8.00 an hour and work 40 hours per week. How much do you make weekly? Monthly? Yearly? How much would you have left if your monthly expenses were spent on rent ($600.00), food ($200.00), transportation ($200.00), and miscellaneous ($270.00)?

6) You have seven classes for which you earned one A, two B's, three C's, and one D. What is your GPA?

7) Lil' Kim is sentenced for five years. She serves 2.5 years and is released. How many days did she serve?

8) You receive $3.00 a day for lunch. You decide to make your lunch and save your money. There are 36 weeks in a school year. How much did you save?

9) You decided to start smoking. A pack of cigarettes costs $6.00. You smoke two packs per week. How much does it cost for the year?

10) Each pack takes two days off your life. If you smoke for 20 years, how many years have you lost?

ANSWERS ARE ON PAGE 134.

# Prison/Jail/Probation

1980—100,000 African American men, 1 of 10

2005—1,500,000 African American men, 1 of 3


1980—30,000 African American women

2005—241,000 African American women


60% of inmate crimes are drug related.


85% of inmates return


Common traits of inmates:


- Illiterate

- High school dropout

- On the corner from 10:00p.m. to 3:00a.m.

- Does not attend church

- Fatherless

❧ ❧ ❧ ❧ ❧ ❧ ❧ ❧ ❧❧ ❧ ❧ ❧ ❧ ❧

1) How can America find $30,000 per inmate but can't find $10,000 for Headstart, Title I, Pell Grants, or job training?

2) How did Malcolm X avoid returning to prison?

3) Are you going to jail?

4) Why are prisons built in the rural area of the state where Whites live?

5) Did you know we could close prisons down if we refused to return?

# Racial Profiling

- Keep your hands out of your pockets when in stores.

- Don't run at night—unless you're being chased.

- When you get in a car, check to make sure the driver has a license, insurance, and vehicle registration. Check for guns and drugs in the glove compartment, under the seat, and in the trunk.

- Understand that store owners will watch you more if you are with your homies.

- When the police pulls you over, this is not the time to be macho. We must make a distinction between a battle and a war. Be respectful, say yes sir or ma'am. Ask permission to move your hands, give good eye contact, and remember the officer's badge number.

- Try to control your emotions. Don't let anyone provoke you.

- Remember, most crimes are committed between 10:00pm and 3:00am. Some police officers do not care who they pick up. Many brothers are at the wrong place at the wrong time.

❧ ❧ ❧ ❧ ❧ ❧ ❧ ❧ ❧❧ ❧ ❧ ❧ ❧ ❧ ❧ ❧

1) Have you ever been a victim of racial profiling?
2) Describe.
3) How can we stop this problem?

# Battle vs. War

- A battle is when you choose not to control your emotions.

- A war is a necessity.

- When someone brushes against you, should you retaliate and be suspended from school (battle) or walk away (war)?

- A teacher is getting on your last nerve. Should you say something (battle), or should you be quiet (war)?

- The police pulls you over, and you know it's harassment. Should you tell them how you feel (battle), or be respectful (war)?

- In a basketball playoff game, the opposing team knows that the other team's star player responds emotionally to provocation (battle). They use their worst player to foul him hard. The star responds by fighting (battle). He's ejected and as a result, is not around to help his team win (war).

- In the *Godfather*, the four families knew Sonny was hot headed and did not know the distinction between a battle and a war. They set him up and killed him. The youngest son, Michael, knew the difference.

- In the movie *Ragtime*, starring Richard Rollins, racists damaged his car (battle). Rollins fought them, lost his car, life, wife, and child (war).

- In the movie *Crash*, a couple is pulled over by the police. The officer abuses his wife (battle). The husband chooses not to respond but gets his badge number and calls his supervisors in the morning (war).

# NBA

- How do you feel about the age limit being raised to 19?

- Why is there no age limit in tennis, hockey, baseball, and golf?

- Why does the NFL require two years after high school graduation?

- What are the career options for a brother who skips college, goes pro, and is cut from the team or incurs a career ending injury?

- Has LeBron James, Kobe Bryant, Kevin Garnett, Jermaine O'Neal, Tracy McGrady, Omare Stoudamire, and Rashard Lewis been good for the NBA?

- Is this a racist idea?

- Is the NBA looking out for the long-term interest of players?

- Should the military raise their limit to 19?

- 1,000,000 boys/girls want to be in the NBA/WNBA.

- Only 400,000 make their high school team.

- Only 4,000 make their college team.

- Only 35 make the NBA.

- Only seven become starters.

- Four years is the average NBA career.

- Three years is the average NFL career.

- Five years is the average baseball career.

- Eighty-six percent of NBA players are African American.

- Two percent of doctors are African American.

ુ  ુ  ુ  ુ  ુ  ુ  ુ  ુ  ુુ  ુ  ુ  ુ  ુ  ુ  ુ

1) Are you going pro?
2) In what sport?
3) What is your backup career?
4) Are you better in sports or science, music or math, rap or reading?

# Dating

- Do most sisters like cool or academic brothers?

- Is it okay for a sister to ask a brother out?

- Are brothers only after sex?

- Do males and females view sex differently? If so, how?

- If it's okay for a brother to "mess around," is it okay for a sister to do the same?

- When should a couple have sex for the first time? First date? Third date? Marriage?

- Who should pay for the date?

- Do sisters respect their sisters' relationships?

- Should sisters fight over a brother?

- Do most brothers lie?

- Can a brother be faithful?

# Sexuality

- What is a menstrual cycle?

- When does it begin?

- When does a boy produce sperm?

- What is abstinence?

- What is an STD?

- List them.

- How can a person claim they are a virgin with an STD or AIDS?

- How can you call yourself a virgin while performing oral sex?

- Did you know 43 percent of HIV positive males are African American?

- Did you know 64 percent of HIV positive females are African American?

- Why is AIDS declining in the White homosexual community and increasing in the Black heterosexual community?

- Sixty percent of teen pregnancy occurs between females ages 11-16 and males ages 17-25.

- Did you know that when you have sex, you sleep with your partner's history?

# Sexually Transmitted Diseases (STDs)

| | |
|---|---|
| Chancroid | A treatable bacterial infection that causes painful sores. |
| Chlamydia | A treatable bacterial infection that can scar the fallopian tubes, affecting a woman's ability to have children. |
| Crabs | Also known as pediculosis pubis, crabs are parasites or bugs that live on the pubic hair in the genital area. |
| Gonorrhea | A treatable bacterial infection of the penis, vagina, or anus that causes pain, or a burning feeling as well as a pus-like discharge. Also known as "the clap." |
| Hepatitis | A disease that affects the liver. There are more than four types. A and B are the most common. |
| Herpes | A recurrent skin condition that can cause skin irritations in the genital region (anus, vagina, penis). |
| Human Papillomavirus (HPV)/Genital Warts | A virus that affects the skin in the genital area, as well as a female's cervix. Depending on the type of HPV involved, symptoms can be in the form of wart-like growths or abnormal cell changes. |

| | |
|---|---|
| Molluscum Contagiosum | A skin disease that is caused by a virus, usually leaving lesions or bumps. |
| Nongonococcal Urethritis (NGU) | A treatable bacterial infection of the urethra (the tube within the penis) often associated with chlamydia. |
| Pelvic Inflammatory Disease (PID) | An infection of the female reproductive organs by chlamydia, gonorrhea, or other bacteria. |
| Scabies | A treatable skin disease that is caused by a parasite. |
| Syphilis | A treatable bacterial infection that can spread throughout the body and affect the heart, brain, nerves. Also known as "syph." |
| Vaginitis | Caused by different germs including yeast and trichomoniasis, vaginitis is an infection of the vagina resulting in itching, burning, vaginal discharge, and an odd odor. |

❧ ❧ ❧ ❧ ❧ ❧ ❧ ❧ ❧❧ ❧ ❧ ❧ ❧ ❧ ❧

1) How can you avoid these diseases?
2) Do you know anyone who has one?
3) Will this happen to you?
4) Did you know you could incur an STD or AIDS with oral sex?

# HIV-AIDS

- You sleep with more than a person. You sleep with your partner's history.

- In the United States, half of all new HIV infections occur in people under age 25, one-fourth in people under the age of 21.

- Because many sexually experienced teens have not been tested for HIV, the actual number of teens living with HIV infection is estimated to be much higher than the reported number.

- Among youth 13 to 19 years old, 57 percent of reported HIV infections occurred among young women and 43 percent among young men.

- In a new study, 93 percent of HIV-infected Blacks were unaware of their infection. Seventy-one percent of those with recognized HIV infection said it was very unlikely that they were infected; 42 percent believed there was little chance they would ever be infected.

- Research suggests that adolescents rarely use condoms or other barriers during oral sex since many consider it to be either "safer sex" or abstinence.

- Among high school students, 61 percent of Black youth reported having had sexual intercourse.

- In a study of African American women ages 13 to 19, 26 percent felt little control over whether or not a condom was used during intercourse; 75 percent agreed that if a male knew a female was taking oral contraceptives, he would not want to use a condom; 66 percent felt that a male partner would be hurt, insulted, or suspicious if asked about his HIV risk factors.

- For many women, negotiating condom use also seems to question trust and fidelity. In one study, African American teenage women felt that not using a condom with a steady partner was a symbol of trust in their partner and the relationship. Moreover, considering asking a partner to wear a condom sometimes brought up fear of rejection or violence.

જ્જ     જ્જ     જ્જ     જ્જ     જ્જ     જ્જ     જ્જ     જ્જ     જ્જજ્જ     જ્જ     જ્જ     જ્જ     જ્જ     જ્જ     જ્જ

1)   What is the difference between HIV and AIDS?
2)   What is the best way to avoid AIDS?
3)   Do you know someone with AIDS?

# Terrible Trick

**Body**    Due to hormone injections in meat and increased cow's milk consumption, males and females are capable of producing a baby earlier than ever before.

**Mind**    Adulthood is based on acquired information. This used to be secured with the written word. Today, electronic media is the major source. Young people now think they are adults because of what they have learned from television.

**Economy**    Farming—Men and women married at 14.
Factory—Men and women married at 16.
Computer—Men and women now marry at 25 or later.

**Terrible Trick**    The body is ready for sex, the mind has seen 100,000 sexual acts by age 18, but the economy says you are not financially capable of taking care of your children.

1) What do you think of this trick?
2) Can you wait sexually until you can take care of your child?
3) Is it fair that your parents or the government have to take care of your child?

# Health

- Did you know you are what you eat?

- Do you read the labels on the food you eat?

- Did you know if you eat three times a day you should eliminate the same number?

- Did you know pork stays 14 days, beef 12, chicken eight, fish five, and fruit and vegetables six hours?

- Did you know your body is 80 percent water?

- How much water do you drink?

- Did you know one of two Americans will die of heart disease?

- Did you know one of three Americans will die of cancer?

- Did you know one of six Americans will die of diabetes?

- Did you know females have started their menstrual cycle six months earlier since 1930 due to lack of breastfeeding and hormones injected in animals?

- How long do you want to live?

- What quality of life do you want to have?

- Will your diet achieve your goal?

# Black Economics

- Write down all the businesses within a two-block radius from your house.

- How many are liquor stores?

- How many are fast food restaurants?

- How many are crack houses?

- How many are owned by African Americans?

- How many are owned by foreigners?

- Who is the largest employer?

- Why do you think your business community looks different from an affluent White business community?

# Wealth

- Why are there more luxury cars in the ghetto than in the suburbs? The average African American has wealth of $10,000. The average White American has wealth of $90,000. Many African Americans buy cars and jewelry, while many Whites buy houses and stocks.

- One youth buys Nike stock, another buys Nike shoes. Which will have the greatest value in one year?

- Why would someone kill someone over a pair of Nike shoes made overseas for $2.38?

- The three most frequent ways to become rich are entrepreneurship, real estate, and the stock market.

- Secure a copy of a business plan.

- Read about housing in foreclosure that you could resell.

- Learn to read the stock pages. Imagine buying a stock and monitor its growth for a year.

- Learn Rule 72. (72) divided by your rate of return is the number of years it will take to double your money. For example, if you had $10,000 and a rate of return of 12 percent (stock market); then 72 divided by 12 = 6. It would only take six years for your $10,000 to become $20,000.

# Hip Hop and Athletic Wealth
# 40 Richest Under 40

| | |
|---|---|
| #13 Sean Combs (P. Diddy) | $315 million |
| #14 Tiger Woods | $295 million |
| #16 Shawn Carter (Jay-Z) | $286 million |
| #22 Shaq O'Neal | $222 million |
| #26 Will Smith | $188 million |
| #40 Kevin Garnett | $106 million |

Source: Fortune Magazine 2004

- P.S. The Godfather of Hip Hop, Russell Simmons, who is over 40 years of age, is worth $500 million.

# The Economics of Education

A high school dropout earns $6.00 per hour.

A high school graduate earns $8.00 per hour.

A college graduate earns $20.00 per hour.

How much does each earn if they work 40 hours?

|  | Weekly | Monthly | Annually |
|---|---|---|---|
| H.S. dropout | _____ | _____ | _____ |
| H.S. graduate | _____ | _____ | _____ |
| College graduate | _____ | _____ | _____ |

ℰ ℰ ℰ ℰ ℰ ℰ ℰ ℰ ℰ ℰ ℰ ℰ ℰ ℰ ℰ ℰ

1) Do you think it's worth staying in school?

2) How much more will a college graduate earn over a high school dropout weekly? Monthly? Annually? Forty years?

95

# Blue Collar Hourly Wages

| | |
|---|---|
| Painters | $15.00 |
| Highway Construction | $18.00 |
| Crane Operators | $20.00 |
| Truck Drivers | $21.00 |
| Carpenters | $22.00 |
| DryWaller | $24.00 |
| Carpet Installers | $24.00 |
| Plumbers | $30.00 |
| Electricians | $31.00 |

1)  Do you have a blue-collar skill?
2)  Would you like to learn one?
3)  Do you know anyone with these skills?

# Strategies to Avoid Being Unemployed

- Earn a good education.

- Become computer literate.

- Communicate well.

- Master computers.

- Learn a blue collar skill.

- Sell legal products that you like.

- Start a business.

- Be willing to volunteer to learn a skill. Never waste your time.

- Be willing to start at the bottom and move to the top.

# Military

- Should the military raise their limit to 19?

- African-Americans are 12 percent of the general population but make up 21 percent of military personnel and 30 percent of Army enlistees.

- "If our great nation becomes involved in an all-out war, the sacrifice must be equally shared," said Rep. Charles B. Rangel, a Black Democrat from New York and a Korean War veteran who opposes military action in Iraq.

❧ ❧ ❧ ❧ ❧ ❧ ❧ ❧ ❧❧ ❧ ❧ ❧ ❧ ❧ ❧

1) Will you volunteer?
2) Would you volunteer if you had other economic alternatives?
3) Is it true the military will help "you be all you can be?"
4) If President Bush was concerned about weapons of nuclear destruction, why didn't the U.S. invade North Korea?

# Goals and Choices

- List a different legal career for each letter of the alphabet. (exclude sports and entertainment).

- What is the difference between a job and career?

- What college will you attend?

- What will be your major?

- What will be your career on your 30th birthday?

- Did you know that what you do in the next four years will determine the next 40 years of your life?

- If you could only choose one, which would it be?
  - A. The finest car available
  - B. All the clothes you could wear
  - C. A mansion
  - D. Time
  - E. 100,000 acres of land
  - F. 1 million dollars

# Time Management

- I pray you chose time. When you leave this earth, you will leave with a car in the garage, clothes in the closet, a house on the block, and money in the bank, but no more time.

- I have studied great people. Whether you are Black or White, male or female, everyone starts with 24 hours.

- Tupac only lived 26 years.

- Martin Luther King, Jr. and Malcolm X only lived to age 39.

- It is not how *long* you live but how *well*.

- Do you waste time?

- What do you do after school?

- How do you spend your weekends?

- If you want to be great, create a 24 hour daily schedule and record how you spend your time.

# School Culture vs. Black Culture

|           I           |           WE          |
| :-------------------: | :-------------------: |
|      Competition      |      Cooperation      |
|       Academics       |       Sports/Rap      |

- School encourages you to be on the honor roll, and take advanced classes.

- Black culture discourages the above and reinforces sports and rap.

- School says tell an adult when someone hits you.

- Black culture says hit them back.

- What are the options?

❧ ❧ ❧ ❧ ❧ ❧ ❧ ❧ ❧❧ ❧ ❧ ❧ ❧ ❧ ❧ ❧

1) How can you avoid fighting?
2) Can you walk away?
3) Can you handle your associates calling you a punk?
4) Can you be in advanced classes and remain cool with your friends?

# Peer Pressure

- Did you know the group you "run" with will be the group you "end" with?

- What is the difference between a friend and an associate?

- A friend would never backstab, lie, or set you up.

- List your friends.

- List your associates.

- If you feel good about yourself, you are less influenced by peer pressure.

- If you are weak, you will be highly influenced by peer pressure.

- Why do some youth think being smart is acting White?

- How do you act Black?

- How do you speak Black?

- Do White students associate being smart with acting Black? Why not?

- Could you leave your friends and tell them you have to go home and study for a test?

- If you were at a party and liquor and hard drugs were passed around, and your friends took some, could you say no?

- Describe one time when you knew what you were doing was wrong, but because your friends were doing it, you continued with them.

# Female Rites of Passage

1)   What is the difference between a female, a girl, and a woman?

2)   When do you become a woman?

3)   What will you be doing when you are 30 years of age?

4)   How do you feel about your hair, complexion, and eye color?

5)   How do you feel about how African American females are portrayed in rap videos?

# Male Rites of Passage

1) What is the difference between a male, a boy, and a man?

2) When do you become a man?

3) Are girls smarter than boys? If so, why?

4) If you were with a group of males, and they wanted to bother a female, how would you respond?

5) Why do mothers stay with their children more than fathers?

6) What will you be doing when you are 30 years of age?

# Boyhood to Manhood

Girls/Boys are students.  Women/Men are teachers.

Girls/Boys are consumers.  Women/Men are producers.

Girls/Boys play with toys.  Women/Men work with tools.

Girls/Boys break things.  Women/Men make things.

Girls/Boys take things apart.  Women/Men put things together.

Girls/Boys ask questions.  Women/Men give answers.

Girls/Boys introduce chaos.  Women/Men bring order.

Girls/Boys run in gangs.  Women/Men organize in teams.

Girls/Boys play house.  Women/Men build homes.

Girls/Boys shack up.  Women/Men get married.

Girls/Boys make babies.  Women/Men raise children.

Girls/Boys won't raise their own children.  Women/Men will raise theirs and somebody else's.

Girls/Boys invent excuses for failure.  Women/Men manufacture strategies for success.

Girls/Boys are self-centered.  Women/Men are other-directed.

Girls/Boys look for somebody to take care of them. Women/Men look for somebody to take care of.

Girls/Boys want popularity.  Women/Men command respect.

Girls/Boys are present centered.  They are up on the latest. Women/Men are time-balanced. They are down with the greatest.

Women/Men have knowledge of the past, understanding of the present, and a vision for the future.

જી  જી  જી  જી  જી  જી  જી  જી  જીજી  જી  જી  જી  જી  જી  જી

1)  Are you a boy or a man?
2)  Are you a girl or a woman?

# Fatherhood

1920—90 percent of African American youth had fathers in the home.

1960—80 percent of African American youth had fathers in the home.

2005—32 percent of African American youth have fathers in the home.

What happened?

Five types of fathers:

1. Sperm donors – stays 18 seconds

2. No show – unfulfilled promises

3. Ice Cream – buys things, goes places, but no chores or responsibilities

4. Step-Dad – very responsible, willing to take care of someone else's responsibility

5. Dad-Father – stays 18 plus years

❧ ❧ ❧ ❧ ❧ ❧ ❧ ❧ ❧❧ ❧ ❧ ❧ ❧ ❧ ❧

1) Which type of dad will you be?

2) Do you know any sperm donors?

3) Do you know any fathers?

Do you see the impact and power a job can have on the family? Write a paper about this photo.

How can a man propose to a woman, marry, and raise a family without a job?

Is fatherlessness the greatest problem in the Black community?

What are the economic options as more manufacturing plants close?

# Physical/Mental/Spiritual

- Are you stronger physically, mentally, or spiritually?

- Most males are stronger physically.

- Are girls smarter than boys?

- Are there more females in college than males?

- Do females go to church more than males?

- Do you measure strength based on bench pressing or staying with your children?

- Who stays with the children the most, mothers or fathers?

- How many push ups can you do?

- How many A's did you earn on your report card?

- How many scriptures do you know?

- Ideally you should be equally strong in all three areas.

# Playing the Race Card

- Two males, one White and one Black, fight. The Black male is suspended and the White male is warned. Was the race card played?

- When your teacher wants you to do your best and will only pass you if you do satisfactory work, should you play the race card?

- When an African American wants to leave college and anonymously writes a racist letter to African Americans, appearing to be white threatening their lives, was she playing the race card?

- When 10 Black males walk in a store, should the owner play the race card?

# African vs. Negro History

- African history began five million years ago.
- Negro history started in 1620.
- African history covers the world.
- Negro history covers the United States.
- African history promotes liberation.
- Negro history promotes docility.
- 2800 BC: pyramids built/first doctor Imhotep.
- 2000 BC: Queen Hatshepsut, great builder.
- 1200 BC: King Ramses II, our greatest king.
- 800 BC: Africans traveled to Mexico and built pyramids.
- 1620 AD: Africans arrive as slaves in the U.S.
- 1865: Slavery ends.
- 1954: Brown vs. Topeka/Montgomery Boycott.
- 1960s: Black power movement.

1) What month do most schools teach Black history?
2) What month do most schools teach White history?
3) How can we use our history to improve our community?
4) How did we go from pyramids to projects?

Read about Imhotep, Ahmose, Queen Hatshepsut, King Ramses, Queen Nzingha, Harriet Tubman, Marcus Garvey, Martin Luther King, and Malcolm X.

# Black History Questions and Facts

- We know six million Jews died in Germany, but how many Africans died in the slave trade?

- How did Marcus Garvey organize more than a million people without television, cell phones, or the Internet?

- Martin King was more than a dreamer. He earned a High School diploma at 15, college degree at 19, masters at 22, and doctorate at 26.

- It's not how long you live but how productive you are. Tupac only lived to 26, King and Malcolm to 39.

- In 1921, in Tulsa the Black community was bombed and there was a race riot. Three hundred African Americans were killed.

- In 1923, in Rosewood, Florida, hundreds of African Americans were killed by a White mob. Their neighborhood was destroyed, and thousands were evacuated. In 1994, the courts approved reparations of up to $150,000 for each of the nine survivors.

- From 1932 to 1972, 399 African American men were used for a government experiment. They had syphilis, but were not given penicillin. Unfortunately, 128 men died.

- In 1943, 1200 African American soldiers of the 364th infantry of the U.S. Army were slaughtered in Centreville, Mississippi, by the U.S. military police.

- Frederick Douglass was beat repeatedly by slaveowners because he would sneak outside to learn to read.

- Africans did not accept slavery. There were 265 documented revolts. Many jumped off the ship, killed their babies, refused to work, and destroyed tools and crops.

- There is something special about you. **You are the offspring of the ancestors who would not die.** They endured because they knew you would make a difference with your life. Will you?

# Malcolm X

| | |
|---|---|
| 1925 | Born Malcolm Little in Omaha, Nebraska, on May 19 |
| 1931 | Father is murdered by the KKK |
| 1942 | Becomes a street hustler in New York City |
| 1946 | Sentenced to 10 years in prison for robbery |
| 1948 | Begins to educate himself while in prison |
| 1949 | Begins correspondence with Elijah Muhammad; converts to the Nation of Islam and changes his name to Malcolm X |
| 1952 | Paroled from prison |
| 1953 | Appointed a minister of the Nation of Islam in Boston |
| 1954 | Appointed a minister of the Nation of Islam's temple in New York City |
| 1958 | Marries Betty X |

| 1962 | Appointed national minister of the Nation of Islam |
|------|---------------------------------------------------|
| 1964 | Breaks with Nation of Islam and founds Muslim Mosque, Incorporated; makes religious pilgrimage to the Middle East; founds Organization of Afro-American Unity; goes on speaking tour of Africa |
| 1965 | Assassinated in New York City on February 21 |

---

- He was born Malcolm Little.

- A racist teacher's comment turned him into Detroit Red.

- Elijah Muhammad turned him into Malcolm X while in prison.

- Malcolm turned himself into El Hajj Malik Shabazz.

❧ ❧ ❧ ❧ ❧ ❧ ❧ ❧ ❧ ❧❧ ❧ ❧ ❧ ❧ ❧ ❧

1) What can we learn from Malcolm's life?

2) What changes are you making in your life?

# Youth in the Movement

- "Each generation out of relative obscurity must discover their mission, fulfill it or betray it." Frantz Fanon

- Youth during slavery jumped off the ship, broke tools, and ran away to freedom.

- Youth fought against Jim Crow laws, sat at White only lunch counters, marched, and picketed.

- Youth in Soweto, South Africa, protested against schools teaching them in an oppressive language.

- Would you boycott Nike, Rebok, Pepsi, Coke, or any other company if necessary?

- What will be your legacy?

- Read Jeremiah 29:11. God has a great plan for your life!

# From a Chicken to an Eagle

There was an eagle one day who lost an egg. The egg was found by a little mother hen who took the eagle egg home with her to the chicken coop and sat on it with all the loving patience of a soon-to-be-mother.

After many days, the little eagle hatched out of the egg. On that very day of his arrival into this world he was, by every measurement, definition, and estimation of the word, an eagle. He was an eagle genetically, an eagle genealogically, an eagle anatomically, and an eagle physiologically. But he was born in chicken circumstances and raised up in a chicken environment; therefore he grew up believing that he was a chicken. He grew up playing chicken games, thinking chicken thoughts, dreaming chicken dreams, walking a chicken walk and talking chicken talk. When the counselor at the chicken high school asked him what he wanted to be when he grew up, he said his greatest ambition was to some day hop, skip and jump up on a fence post and cock-a-doodle-do fo' day like he saw the roosters do.

Now, the chickens that he lived among got together and planned to wage psychological warfare against him behind his back. Why? Because they knew who he really was. They got together when he wasn't around and said to one another, "If he ever finds out that he's an eagle, us chickens are in trouble!"

So they did everything they could to make him ashamed of his eagle self. They were determined to rob him of his eagle self-esteem. They laughed at him, called him names, and pointed fingers of scorn at him. They made him the butt of their jokes and the target of their ridicule. They made fun of his eagle features. They called his large, powerful, curvaceous, intimidating eagle beak ugly and said that he was deformed. But in fact, they were just jealous because they had little-bitty, thin chicken lips. They poked fun at his razor sharp, steel strong, eagle talons, but it was because they had weak, puny, pitiful chicken feet.

After so many years of being bombarded with negative messages about himself, that little lost bird began to feel ashamed of himself. He even considered making an appointment with a cosmetic surgeon to have his talons reduced and half of his beak cut off so he could look more like and fit in better with the chickens.

One day, while the lost bird was playing in the barnyard, he saw the dark contours of a mighty shadow float across the ground like some great ship swimming across the restless bosom of yonder's mighty oceans. For the first time in his life he looked up, higher than the chicken coop, higher than the fence post, higher than the line of trees that ringed his chicken environment. And he saw, framed against the sundrenched afternoon sky, the regal form of an adult eagle in full flight, with all the power, beauty, grace, rhythm, and majesty of that king of the air. It seemed as if his mighty wings filled the sky, blotted out the sun, and stretched from horizon to horizon. When that little lost eagle beheld the fantastic sight of the adult bird, his mind was blown. He was so startled that he exclaimed to himself deep down in the innermost recesses of his heart of hearts: "Boy, I sho' wish I could be like that!" But then he remembered that they told him at the chicken high school that his I.Q. was too low and his SAT scores weren't high enough for him to entertain exalted ambitions for his future. So he dropped his head in sorrow and despair.

But the adult eagle, with the accuracy of his long-range, binocular vision saw the lost bird. With the wisdom that comes from many years, he perceived his dilemma. He then swooped down from his stratospheric height, landed next to the little lost bird, walked up to him, looked him in the eye, and said, "Boy, you ain't no chicken. You are an eagle! Your mighty talons were not meant to grub and scrub along the lowlands of the earth for worms and caterpillars, but to grab hold to the craggy sides of fierce mountains of mighty achievements. Boy, did you hear what I said? You ain't no chicken, you are an eagle. Your eagle eyes were never meant to be limited to the narrow confines of the barnyard, but to seek out the distant panoramic horizons of your own unfulfilled potential. Boy, spread your wings and be caught up in the wafting winds of your own immeasurable genius."

The moral of his story is
For those that don't know
We are not a chicken people.
We are a race of eagles.
So even if you have to attend
Some chicken schools,
And even if you have
Some chicken teachers,
Who make you read chicken books,
And even if you have to work
On some chicken jobs
Under some chicken supervisors
Who give you chicken assignments
And pay you chicken money

Don't do chicken work
And don't bring home no
Chicken grades
'Cause you ain't no chicken
You are an eagle!

by Clarence James

1) Are you a chicken or an eagle?
2) Do you act like an eagle?
3) Do you have eagle friends?

# Attitude

The longer I live, the more I realize the impact of attitude on life. Attitude, to me, is more important than facts. It is more important than the past, than education, than money, than circumstances, than failures, than success, than what other people think or say or do. It is more important than appearance, gifts, or skills. It will make or break a company...a church...a home. The remarkable thing is we have a choice every day regarding the attitude we will embrace for that day. We cannot change our past...we cannot change the fact that people will act in a certain way. We cannot change the inevitable. The only thing we can do is pray on the one string we have, and that is our attitude. I am convinced that life is 10 percent what happens to me and 90 percent how I react to it.

❧ ❧ ❧ ❧ ❧ ❧ ❧ ❧ ❧❧ ❧ ❧ ❧ ❧ ❧ ❧

1)  What grade would you give yourself on attitude?
2)  How can you improve your attitude?

# Values

Nguzo Saba

1. Unity

2. Self-determination

3. Collective work and responsibility

4. Cooperative economics

5. Purpose

6. Creativity

7. Faith

Ma'at

1. Truth

2. Justice

3. Order

4. Harmony

5. Balance

6. Reciprocity

7. Righteousness

1) Do you value I or we?

2) Do you value competition or cooperation?

3) Can you be trusted?

4) Do you lie?

5) Do you steal?

6) Do you buy "hot" goods and bootleg CDs and videos?

7) Do you think that increases crime?

8) Do you respect elders?

9) Will you be faithful to your mate?

10) Will you stay with your children?

11) Could you kill someone other than for self-defense?

# SAT Scores

Are you going to college?

America is a test-taking country.

## SAT Averages

| | |
|---|---|
| Asians | 1083 |
| White | 1063 |
| Hispanics | 900 |
| African American | 857 |

What are the reasons for the gap?

Poverty?

Single parents?

Low teacher expectations?

School funding?

Cultural bias of tests?

Low study time?

## Study Time Per Week

| | |
|---|---|
| Asians | 12 hours |
| Whites | 8 hours |
| Hispanics | 5 hours |
| African American | 4 hours |

African American youth:

Watch 38 hours of television

Listen to 18 hours of rap

Talk on the telephone 11 hours

Spend 9 hours playing

Whatever you do **most** will be what you do **best**!

Do you study more than you watch television? Listen to music? Talk on the telephone? Play?

# Test-Taking Techniques

1) Relax and encourage yourself throughout the exam. Tell yourself that you will earn a great score.

2) Get a good night sleep before the test.

3) Stay relaxed; if you begin to get nervous take a few deep breaths slowly to relax yourself and then get back to work.

4) Read the directions slowly and carefully.

5) If you don't understand the directions on the test, if possible, ask the teacher to explain.

6) Skim through the test so that you have a good idea how to pace yourself.

7) Write down important formulas, facts, definitions, and/or keywords in the margin first so you won't worry about forgetting them.

8) A student scored 79 when told it was a test and scored 121 when told it was a game. Think of the test as a game.

9) Finish the exam. Answer all questions, even if you have to guess.

10) Never stop for a long time on a question. Place a dot next to the question, and return if time permits. Answer the easy questions first.

11) Read all answers before deciding. The first answer has the least probability and the last answer has the greatest. If you choose the first answer without reading all of them, you will not realize that the last answer included the first.

12) Use the process of elimination. There are five answers, and probably three of them do not make sense. You have a 50 percent probability with the remaining two answers.

13) Before reading the answers, ask yourself what the question is asking. Determine your answer first and then look for it in the answer key. Do not let multiple answers confuse you.

14) When in doubt, go with your first intuition.

15) Avoid careless mistakes. Place your answer in the right box. If time permits, check your work. Use all the time available. You do not score higher because you finished first.

16) Qualifiers like *never, always,* and *every* mean that the statement must be true all of the time. Usually these types of qualifiers lead to a false answer.

17) If any part of the question is false, then the entire statement is false, but just because part of a statement is true doesn't necessarily make the entire statement true.

18) Every part of a true sentence must be true. If any one part of the sentence is false, the whole sentence is false, despite many other true statements.

19) Pay close attention to negatives, qualifiers, absolutes, and long strings of statements.

20) Negatives can be confusing. If the question contains negatives, such as *no, not,* and *cannot* drop the negative and read what remains. Decide whether that sentence is true or false. If it is true, it's opposite, or negative, is usually false.

21) Qualifiers are words that restrict or open up general statements. Words like *sometimes, often, frequently, ordinarily,* and *generally* open up the possibilities of making accurate statements. They make more modest claims, are most likely to reflect reality, and usually indicate true answers.

22) Absolute words restrict possibilities. *No, never, none, always, every, entirely,* and *only* imply the statement must be true 100 percent of the time and usually indicate false answers.

23) Long sentences often include groups of words set off by punctuation. Pay attention to the truth of each of these phrases. If one is false, it usually indicates a false answer.

24) In "All of the above" and "None of the above" choices, if you are certain one of the statements is true, don't choose "None of the above." If one of the statements are false, don't choose "All of the above."

25) In a question with an "All of the above" choice, if you see at least two correct statements, then "All of the above" is probably the answer.

26) If there is an "All of the above" option and you know that at least two of the choices are correct, select the "All of the above" choice.

27) Usually the correct answer is the choice with the most information.

28) Look for key words in test directions and questions such as: *choose, describe, explain, compare, identify, similar, except, not,* and *but.*

29) How can you avoid skipping a line on the answer sheet? Use a sheet of paper and line up your answers.

30) Many questions use the following words: *trace, support, analyze, explain, infer, summarize, evaluate, compare, formulate, contrast, describe,* and *predict.* You must know the meanings of these words.

# A Culturally Biased Test for Your Teacher

- What year did Hip Hop and rap begin?

- What is Bling-Bling?

- What is a jimmy hat?

- What is Up North?

- Give one reason why some people think Tupac is still alive?

- Name one Hip Hop clothing line.

- Name one Hip Hop magazine.

- Describe the videos "Tip Drill" and "Candy Shop."

- Who is the hottest male rapper? What do you know about him?

- What was Washington's first name?

- Why do they call him 50 Cent?

# The Bet

- Society is betting that if you are Black, low-income, from a single parent home and a poor neighborhood, and your parent lacks a college education, you will drop out.

- I'm betting that you are going to be a success.

- What do you believe?

- I'm betting you will be successful because I've seen thousands of youth from the above conditions do well. How did they do it? One or more of the following occurred:
  - parent turned off television
  - student became an athlete and the coach became a father figure.
  - student gave his life to Christ.
  - student joined a rites of passage or mentoring program.
  - student was determined not to fail.
  - parent monitored the peer group and idle street time.
  - student found employment and learned discipline.

# Closing Questions

• What have you learned

from this book?

• What will you be doing when you're

30 years of age?

# Answers from pages 52, 74-75

1) 16 / 105 / 60

2) 43%

3) 35%

4) $117.57

5) $320 / $1,280 / $16,640 / $10

6) 2.4

7) 913

8) $540

9) $624

10) You smoked 2 packs per week / 108 per year / 20 years:

    2160 x 2 = 4320 divided by 365 - 12 years lost

### Drug Deaths

8,000 heroin

15,000 cocaine

100,000 alcohol

434,000 nicotine

# Notes

# Notes